INSPIRE

INSPIRE

Motivate and Train
Your Sales Team to
Grow Your Business

Yazmín Torres
PADILLA

NEW YORK

LONDON • NASHVILLE • MELBOURNE • VANCOUVER

Inspire

Motivate and Train Your Sales Team to Grow Your Business

Published in New York, New York, by Morgan James Publishing in partnership with Difference Press. Morgan James is a trademark of Morgan James, LLC. www.MorganJamesPublishing.com

ISBN 9781642794694 paperback
ISBN 9781642794700 eBook
ISBN 9781642796339 audiobook
Library of Congress Control Number: 2019933109

Cover Design by:
Rachel Lopez
www.r2cdesign.com

Interior Design by:
Christopher Kirk
www.GFSstudio.com

Morgan James is a proud partner of Habitat for Humanity Peninsula and Greater Williamsburg. Partners in building since 2006.

Get involved today! Visit
MorganJamesPublishing.com/giving-back

Table of Contents

Introduction

Well, if you are reading this book, it is because you, like many others, have a sales department problem, and you really want to change this fact. I know exactly how you can change things for good.

To show you how, I am going to tell you what Pedro's life was like when I met him.

Pedro was referred by another client of mine, and he called to make an appointment to talk about his need to hire good sellers for his company. When I entered his company, I saw a beautiful and cozy space with some workers around talking to each other, exchanging papers, typing on their computers, and answering their phones. It looked like everyone was busy with a lot of work and really concentrating on the important stuff. We went into his office, and when I sat down I saw a family picture on his desk – it was him with his beautiful wife and his two sons.

I couldn't hold it in, and I said, "You have a really beautiful family." This made him feel very comfortable and proud of that because it was true.

"Well," I said, "tell me what is going on."

He said that he needed to hire some sellers.

I asked, "How many?"

He said, "Two to start, but if they are good workers, I may hire more."

I have heard this sentence many times before, so I knew that behind this affirmation there was a lot more work to be done. You will discover this as you read this book.

"That is good news," I said. "It is more work for me. Okay, let's start defining the seller's profile."

As we were filling the profile format, I was asking some important information like, "Do these sellers need to have any degrees?"

He answered, "Not really. I just need them to know how to sell."

"Mmm, okay," I responded. "Do these sellers need to have experience?"

"Not really. My best seller had no experience when she started working here," he said.

"Well, is this a replacement position?"

"Yes," he said. "We have some rotation in this position because it is difficult to find really committed and efficient people. When I started this business eight years ago, I was aware that I had to act as a General Manager, salesman, and concierge, but after all these years, it seems to be the same. I am the only one who makes really good deals with clients. Most of the sellers I hired have not generated higher results."

"I understand," I said, knowing he may have tried some other solutions before without success. "Please tell me more about your sales department and the troubles you are suffering."

"Basically, I am having a hard time finding sellers that make my business grow. The rotation is affecting the satisfaction of my clients, and the workers of this area aren't self-motivated to work hard. They are always complaining about the amount of work they have or the goals I set for them."

I am going to pause here! Your story might be pretty similar to Pedro's, and you are nodding your head saying, "Yes, I understand Pedro's feelings!"

Here is a summary of what has happened so far:

Most Owners' Problems with the Commercial Department:

1. The difficulty of finding good sellers to hire
2. The time spent thinking everything is going to be different someday
3. The owner is the person who makes good income for the company
4. The rotation is affecting client satisfaction
5. The sellers are not self-motivated

Like Pedro, those are real problems for many small to medium company owners.

Now, let's continue with the story.

"I understand," I replied quietly. "Now tell me how you have tried to solve your problem."

"Ufff," he responded with a gesture of fatigue. "I've tried most things that big companies do, like contract Team Buildings, Consultants, and Sales Trainings. Now I am willing to try a recruiter."

Hey, you are very clever! Here is another pause. To be realistic, any recruiter, including me, will fail in this process if the profile is not very well thought out according to what the specific characteristics are that we need for the sales person. Maybe you have already noticed that the profile could not be made just by thinking that any person could become a good seller, as Pedro was not clear on what he was looking for.

Let's recap:

The Solutions That Most Owners Had Tried:

1. Team Buildings
2. Consultants
3. Sales Trainings
4. Recruiters

Dear reader, I want you to know that these four options are totally right to contract but not for those problems we mentioned. I will keep going with the story so you will know why.

"So, Pedro, what were you expecting with those options you contracted as a solution?" I asked.

"Well, what I really want is to increase sales so my company could grow. But I recognize that I need some external help because I have tried on my own for many years, and I feel stuck," he said and let his arms fall down wearily.

Something very important to be aware of, is that the expectation might reveal the reason why the things he tried didn't work.

The Expectation:

He wanted to increase sales so the company could grow.

I kept on investigating: "And what results did you get after those contracted solutions?"

"None of them were long lasting. The effects only lasted a few weeks, and it wasn't cheap," Pedro answered.

I already knew that if I took the job as a recruiter it wouldn't last either. Maybe I could guess very well at what he wanted, and with my experience I could make him hire two good sellers. But by the time they got in, they would immediately be contaminated by the behavior of the other workers.

The Results That Most Owners Had and Will Keep Having with the Contracts He Made:

1. Time wasted
2. Money wasted (sunk cost)
3. No long-lasting results increasing sales

Pedro had these bad experiences with no success. He even told me he wouldn't pay anything until he was totally sure that the people he hired with this recruitment process could make a sales increase.

I really understood his fears. If I was him, I would be feeling that way, too.

Owner's Fears:

1. More money wasted
2. More time wasted
3. More trusting unknown people

I think I need to make something clear: I am not saying that hiring Trainers, Team Buildings, Recruiters, or Consultants is bad decision or a waste of time and money, but the results are not long lasting. You will know how I figured this out if you keep reading.

Chapter One:

My Story

My Childhood

When I was little and someone asked me, "What do you want to be when you grow up?" the only thing that came to my mind was to be an entrepreneur. That was, for me, a synonym of hard work, pride, and lots of money. I wanted to run my own business. My father was the most important example of a businessman. Since he was young, his hard work, vision, honesty, and his ability to make business made him a successful professional. It was because of him that I wanted to be my own boss. He made it seem very easy to accomplish.

My Entry into the Entrepreneurial World

The years passed by, and after I graduated from high school, I started working into a multinational company, thanks to God and to one of my mom's friends. It was a very nice experience. I learned how to work with the formalities of a big company and the sense of belonging to a very exclusive group from where nobody would leave voluntarily.

A few years later, my personal situation - which was being a university student and a single mother – was interfering with my workday. I could not aspire to professional growth without a degree, so I decided to quit and find a part-time job. That was the moment my life was defined as an entrepreneur! I met a very interesting grown-up man; he saw me sitting on the waiting couch of a company where I had an interview. He asked if I was looking for a job, and, immediately, I said, "Yes!"

"Hi, my name is Yazmín" I said.

"I am Leo," he said.

I instantly felt his beautiful soul. "I am here looking for a part time job. Are you the one I am supposed to see today?" I asked.

He said, "Yes, but I am not the person whom you had an appointment with. I don't even work here." He laughed.

"But I saw in your eyes that you are a good worker, and you look like you are good at sales."

I really didn't know what to say, but I kept walking by his side as if I was hypnotized.

He asked the lady at the reception desk for an office so he could have a quiet space to interview me, and she immediately opened one for us.

After some questions about my experience and my reasons for leaving that prestigious company I worked for, I had the chance to get to know him and the job he was interested in hiring me to do.

"Okay, let me explain to you who I am. I am the uncle of the person who was going to interview you. We are starting a new business, and we are hiring someone who can help us to sell the stuff we import," he explained.

I was very happy with the conditions he told me, so I agreed and started to work with them right away.

Two months later, I kept going to the office where I used to work with Leo, and nothing was happening. He and his nephew were busy all the time with his other companies, and I was having a hard time because Leo offered me to earn a quantity of money very like to the one I was earning at that big company. It was a mix between a secure salary and commissions, and there were no products to sell. I was getting very nervous, and I went to talk to him. After some explanations, I decided to look for the products that we were going to import and do all import procedures, customs clearance, sanitary registration, etc. to have the products released to be extended. When I made all that on my own I started selling, but I didn't realize that we didn't have invoices to give to the corporate clients. As a desperate measure, I took some of my invoices, and I gave them to the clients that needed bills to pay us. The checks went out with my name on them, and I ran to change them and give Leo the money to gain my commissions.

After three months of working this way, I felt very happy with what I was doing. Leo was very grateful with my job. But the international and national providers, the clients, and even the guy who rented us the office were asking to talk only with me.

That was the moment when Leo said, "I need to talk to you." I didn't realize until that day that I was the one who was running the whole office, and they didn't have the time to even control what I was doing. Leo's nephew was the CEO, and he never showed up because he was taking care of another business that was more important for him.

Leo said to me, "You are a really entrepreneur! I have noticed that you only needed someone to tell you that you are doing a great job. If we continue like this, you will realize that the business is yours, and it could become a problem for all of us. I could keep on guiding you on whatever you need, and we may contract a seller and an import assistant to keep on trying for an organized company."

He made me see my potential, something I must have learned from my father, and threw me into the independent professionals.

If you are wondering what happened with Leo's business, well, it disappeared. His nephew was very busy with other things, and Leo died very soon after.

Well, here I was with a new situation in my life. I was trying to survive. I started a journey like an entrepreneur, but my head and my time was into my studies and my baby girl. I did enough to live, and it went like that for a few years until I got my psychology degree. All I wanted to do was to start working again in a multinational company because now I had the time and my degree to keep growing. But as a just-graduated person, all I could aspire to was a junior position with a basic salary and a lot of operative work, and I needed more money and time because I was a mother with a lot of responsibilities, not like a junior normally is. Besides, I was used to earning more money because I had my own business.

The Consulting Company

I decided to start a new business. I was going to work by myself on what I had studied, so I started to research about what big consultant companies offered and their common services. I kept studying and training myself. I also hired some important consultants and trainers to make them work for some of my clients and learned any detail I could be missing.

I learned everything I could about the consultant industry so I could have a big port of services to offer to my clients that let me have a team of ten to twenty people working for me. What my company basically did was recruitment, training, team buildings, and consultant services to help companies' owners solve aspects that they and their managers have to adjust. That is the way that the company generates the economic results they expect.

My consulting company worked very well. I was making a lot of money, even though it was a small and not very known company. I learned how to make things exactly as a big consultant company does; I followed the same procedures, and sometimes I hired professionals from these companies to work with me on big projects. But after some years of doing this I found that all consultant companies, even if they were big and recognized or a small business as mine, in most cases did not generate long-term results. When you contract a consultant company to help you increase sales, basically what they do is cover a symptom and not treat the disease.

How I Developed the INSPIRE Business Model Program

After I learned what most big Consulting Companies do only with good intentions but not long-lasting results, life, God, and the universe converged and brought my attention to the needs of a friend. He was running the commercial department of a very recognized company, and he was searching for an HR person who had commercial skills because he needed to develop a very ambitious project. Guess what… That was me! There was my opportunity to start my own way to make things happen.

He was asking me to propose a training methodology for about six-hundred people around the country to develop knowledge and skills almost at the same time without inter-rupting their workday. The most important thing was that he wanted the results to be measured somehow; he wanted a real and permanent impact.

I entered in a very demanding disruptive process, and after a few weeks it finally appeared – a very nice model that covered the needs of my new client and even more.

I created a program that develops the commercial skills and the product knowledge the sellers must have with a short group training in the place where they worked and individual coaching to show them how to implement what they have already learned. I called this program INSPIRE because it is how a business owner could develop and com-municate a pure and well-intentioned labor philosophy that influences others with a sense of urgency or ability to do (your sales team) and feel about something (your clients). That is how this Program can reach all these results.

Benefits of the INSPIRE Business Model Program

1. Redefine the service to generate value for your clients.
2. Teach leaders know how to lead their commercial departments.

3. Train all the sellers and other profiles that have commercial activities to make more sales and keep old clients.
4. Develop equally on every person's commercial skills.
5. Find bottlenecks and common errors.
6. Collect information to develop new products.
7. Decrease workers' rotation.
8. Evaluate staff constantly.
9. Attract and hire good profiles.
10. Reward and maintain only the workers who really make contributions to the company.
11. Measure the impact.
12. Increase sales sustainably.

I have been leading with this model for about five years, watching only success and very happy clients. I was earning a lot of money by charging a recurring fee of the sales I helped make. I kept perfecting while I increased my knowledge by studying around the world and working for different industries.

In these five years as the person whose companies contracted to make them sell more, I noticed that even if the program was the same for every company, they had different behaviors. Some of them acted faster than others and had more benefits without much effort – this was because they implemented the INSPIRE as a culture model.

What I really wanted was to make a change on the company sales results in a long term, stop covering the symptoms, and heal the disease permanently. But I was still the person who they contracted to make things happen, so I kept researching all the companies that made a permanent and an immediate change. I realized that was because the owners were totally into the process and worked hard to make the team follow everything I taught them. In the companies where the results were more successful, I was not the leader – the owner was the leader.

Then I knew that the only way that a company could grow sustainably was the deep intention of the owner or the person who runs the company to make an important change.

This is where I was when I met Pedro, and he was really waiting for a program like this. I taught him everything I knew about the INSPIRE Business Model, and we did it together for some time. He developed the correct inspiring-philosophy to make his workers and clients love the company and services it extended. He became the best manager for his company to grow and increase sales continuously.

Like Pedro, there are other happy owners who could jump from a small size business into a well-recognized company.

The key to achieve this important and gorgeous goal of increasing sales to make your business grow is to become the spokesperson of the inspiringphilosophy. This is why I wanted to write this book: to tell you that only you have the responsibility, the capability, and the honor to make your company grow and have awesome results. I will show you how you can do it by your own. Not falling in a dependent relationship with trainers, consultants, or workers that only generates paying bills. And make it possible in only nine weeks.

I am going to explain to you how to do it.

SEVEN STEPS YOU MIGHT FOLLOW:

1. IDENTIFY YOUR PATH: Remember the reason why you started your business. Who did you want to help? Here is where you develop the inspiringphilosophy that would make your workers and clients feel with – the urge or the ability to do or feel something for your company and the products or services you extend.

2. PROPOSE VALUE: Define what your client really considers worthwhile and helpful, and this

is going to be the breaking point and the reason why he is going to love your product or service. You might know that your company is not the only one doing X to supply the need that your client has, so you must know how competitive the industry your company is in and develop a strategy to deal with issues that make the industry not profitable as you would like, so it generates value for you, too.

3. SERVE WITH LOVE: Be clear on all the characteristics that your client has and make some innovation so he prefers your services and products to those of others. Make a problem-solving offer so every single person at your commercial department knows why you are the best option in the industry. Create a culture of service so your client can have the best experience he could have.

4. INTRIGUE YOUR AUDIENCE: Define the activities that the commercial stuff is going to do and what are the personal characteristics and abilities your sellers need to have so that the goals could be achieved and your clients could be well attended. And use the same marketing strategies you are

going to use for your clients to recruit the best sellers and workers you could have.

5. ENGAGE THEIR PASSION: Create the perfect environment so everybody feels like he or she is part of an exclusive group and give the best of them. They will spread this to your clients.

6. REFINE SKILLS: Everyone in your commercial team needs to develop some skills, so make an equal opportunity to learn about the product or service that your company offers. You can also offer and sell techniques so all of them can achieve rewards to accomplish the goals you set. Make your own training and coaching process so it will be a long-term impact.

7. NORMALIZE PROCEDURES: Create all the formalities your team need to know to make good decisions by themselves and all the formalities you need to get all the information in the right moment to correct anything immediately.

If you make these seven steps part of the culture of the commercial area in your company, you will make your sales increase enough to keep growing. You will jump from a small organization into a well-recognized company.

Chapter Two:

Identify Your Path

I was sitting in front of Pedro, watching his face as it changed from a very worried and demanding expression to a friendly and interested one. He told me that he was willing to learn and change everything so that he could be empowered to grow his company.

It was when I knew it was time to teach him instead of doing it for him because I wanted to make him the best manager he could be and develop the skills he needed to make it happen!

The first step is to analyze why you started your company.

Your Dream Will Become Everybody's Mission:

There are two kinds of entrepreneurs: the ones who start the business because they want to make money, and the ones who had a dream of helping the need of others.

Neither is good or bad, and neither are free from the idea of better incomes. But there is a lot of different implications backwards.

A money-making business is one that only thinks about one person – the owner. We cannot work in a long-lasting company because every strategy will be around how much money we could make for X person. If this person is gone, everything that everyone had worked for will be lost. If you are looking just for money, it is less risky to be an investor and make some investments to make your capital grow.

The companies that emerge from the good intention of helping or making a difference in others lives has a sustainable philosophy. They gather people from everywhere who are touched by this idea. You are going to work with people *for* people. There are a lot of companies in different industries that are good examples. Think about how a non-profit businesses work with volunteers or MLM companies which have strong sellers earning only from his sales. Even big companies like Amazon, Microsoft, Apple, Disney, Nike,

Google, and many others started with the dream of helping people and have been very profitable for a long time and into the foreseeable future. Some of them no longer have the founder alive and are still growing and expanding.

This dream is what we are going to call "The Philosophy" of the company. I am against the traditional way of defining the mission of the company, where some certification companies make you establish in detail what you are producing, where, for whom, why, etc. Those missions limit companies from doing what they dream. Let me show you with some examples:

Looking to help older people in Spain who needed more incomes when the whole country was in a financial crisis, some people were thinking about making projects where elderly could make money. These ideas included taking care of kids or dogs when families need someone to watch them. It was not viable because of the poor health of the older people. They needed to find some way for the elderly to make enough money to pay their bills, like for doctors and insurance.

That is when the idea of a reverse mortgage popped up. This made retired people have enough economical flow to solve their needs without leaving their homes, and also the sons and daughters of these people did not need to send them money or have to move them to a nursing home.

This is an example that good business can be made with good intentions. If they keep the philosophy of helping older people instead of just making profit in the financial industry with a focus strategy, they could develop some more products to cover the needs of this community.

Let analyze Nike's philosophy: "To bring inspiration and innovation to every athlete in the world." They define athlete to everybody who has a body. This type of mission inspires workers. It doesn't narrow your business geographically. It makes the company open to any other business that makes it accomplish this philosophy, and it creates partners that could help them accomplish this mission.

With each of these examples, every business owner could remember and find out the contribution you can make to a certain community or the whole society. The big challenge at this point is to break down the concepts you learned so far about starting a business and get really deep in your selfless intentions to create a business that will bring you a lot of personal and economic gratuity.

Let me tell you a little more about my story. As I told you, when I started my Consultant Company my superficial intention was to have a bigger income than what I was going to get if I had started working for a company. I could not lower my income or my time available for my daughter, and that reason led me to create a company that was the same as every other company, focusing only on having economical results immediately and not risking time and money. This was a selfish reason, but not bad because the truth is that I have to take care of me and my loved ones. But thinking deeply, my new consultant company harbored about twenty workers and attended to a good quantity of companies that had thousands of people on their payroll that really needed their jobs. I was not risking anything for me or for them, but I was not making a substantial difference in the results they got.

After years passed and I noticed that there were not major differences for the employees who worked in my company or worked for other consultant business. For my clients choosing between any option on the market, I accepted that the real reason why I studied so much and I worked so hard was not only for the money – what I really wanted was to help business owners that feel stuck to become the persons who transformed their business to sell more, grow, and expand by inspiring the world. In that moment, I took the risk of developing the INSPIREphilos-ophy, even though I knew most of my clients would not understand the good intention of this business model and, of course, as an original service nobody would know about. I knew I should invest some money in creating awareness.

I know you are thinking that it is a very utopian way of thinking. But this is what will make a real difference for you and the people who surround your company, and it will bring you a lot more economical and personal returns.

Chapter Three:

Propose Value

Knowing that you have a really well-intentioned business in mind, we have to make sure that it generates value for you and your clients.

Analyze and Make Your Dream Profitable:

Entrepreneurs start their business with a lot of positivity, which is very important, but the reasons why they think it might be a good investment are maybe not well studied.

Although Pedro, as many other business owners, had been running his business for some years, he never analyzed if the business was profitable enough to deal with all the everyday issues he had to confront. Sometimes the profitability is better with less effort from being an investor. When he started working on it, he was doing well, but when he wanted to grow, he started losing money and time. Now he knows that he could be doing it better if he found some assertive help. So, it is very important to know in what industry you are competing and what are the conditions in that area.

You have to see how many clients and how many competitors are going to be in the very near future because it depends on how much power you are going to have over your client. For example, imagine you are on a sunny beach and there are a lot of thirsty people around, and you are the only one who has a bottle of water on sale. How much do you think that bottle will cost? But if we change one single aspect of the story, like having a fount of pure water nearby or maybe you're the only person around, your bottle is not going to worth much or maybe even worth nothing.

With this exact example, let's imagine that the situation was very propitious for you to sell your bottle of water at a very high price. Even though you would earn a lot of money, to get or create a new bottle of water would be very difficult because you cannot find a supplier there, so you have to invest almost everything you earn in a flight to get a new one. Then your profit would be very low. Do you still think that it is a good business to invest in? There are some business that seem to be very interesting until you make a deep analysis. There are some other aspects you might analyze – like maybe you are the only one who has water for sale, but there is another guy who sells Gatorade.

A lot of companies just want to sell more, and they don't even notice that they are selling bottles of water when there is a free fountain nearby. But don't worry because if you know what the conditions are that your company is involved in, then you can generate ideas to counteract the problems that your company might have to face up front.

This is a process you must do with someone who really masters the tools and the subject well, to make a good analysis and define the best strategy. I had the best mentor on the topic of business analysis during my MBA studies and used to apply this for my clients, with incredible results. It took me a few years to realize that I could make this analysis for my own business. I was earning enough money, so I thought I didn't need it. The truth is that every business owner should make this analysis because the probability of creating the most favorable results for the investment of time and money is going to be way more profitable than what is now.

What I realized with the analysis I did on my own was that I unconsciously adopted a wrong strategy for my business; even though I was making a lot of money, I was losing a lot of money that I could make. My company used to attend clients from all types of industries. Most of the clients were companies that were used to contracting these kinds of services, so they had the power to make us, the competitors, get into a price war. I was sacrificing a big portion of earnings because I was a small company and I had to lower my price.

The INSPIRE Business Model Program, that was created selflessly with all the good intention of making a true and long-term change on the results business owners had, was the service that could get me off that bad strategy I chose. I changed my client's results and my own running program, I expanded my company, and now I attend to clients around the world because no other company has the program I developed.

How to Develop a Value Proposition:

Now that you are clear on what your dream is and how you can make it an interesting and profitable business, you must validate what you think is what your client really considers valuable so you can focus your energy on the important.

You must detail all your client characteristics to identify every aspect where you can generate a value proposition, or you can do an innovation activity to improve the offer you make above the competition. Remember, your client is going to buy what he thinks is worth it. This is the way not only the client is going to be happy but also your sellers. It is going to be easier and more gratifying.

For example, thinking again of my old Consultant Company, when I was working with the traditional business model I was doing things very similarly to other companies. My client really didn't get any difference between me and my competitors. But when I focused on truly helping my clients, I understood that what they really appreciated was:

- The possibility to learn how they could get the results they were looking for and turning into the professional that could achieve the goals on their own so they won't depend on others and save money
- To get them long-term incredible results, making them transform their stuck business in a growing company

- To make this possible in only nine weeks; my clients really appreciate the time they save making things happen fast

So, to make sure you understand this part well, I am going to show you another value proposition that a well-known company offers to their clients. Remember that the value proposition is only for their target – if it doesn't seem important to you, it's okay, but think about how these characteristics made them get more clients and be preferred over other competitors.

For example:

- Airbnb: They develop this incredible company thinking of the benefits of everybody, with an inspiringphilosophy that is to "help others live in this world where they can feel like home is anywhere." They really generate value for their clients, creating a community where people who travel can find:

  1. Places where their clients feel at home
  2. Lots of options with different prices around the world
  3. Recommended activities while you are staying at some specific places

These three values are things that have shaken the hotel industry and guarantee Airbnb an interesting income.

The Resources and Activities You Must Check Out:

After you defined and developed what is going to be your value proposition, it is a must that you have to control everything related to the client satisfaction generating process. If it is related to a provider, an exclusive area, or to a specific activity, you should be sure that it is working perfectly.

For example, in my case I offer my client that he could learn everything he needs to become the person who transforms his own business into a growing company by inspiring the world. I have to make sure that the main activity my company has is very well developed so that it is giving the client all the knowledge and support that he needs. Also, it is very important that I share this information to make this activity possible. Maybe I have to hire a web developer to make a website where I can upload videos so every client around the world could see, or I can have a strategy partner to make this possible, or I could pay for a provider that has this service.

In Airbnb's case, they offer the possibility of getting a place like home in most parts of the world, so they have to create the network to make this happen and to make sure that the places they offer are good enough. They have developed an awareness system to generate all their leads and providers. Control that all these people are secure with their transactions and with their experiences. One of the resources they may have is a good website with the capability to expand as needed. In addition, a procedure to secure the experience and control who is going to use an Airbnb place and who is hosting an Airbnb to ensure the safety of the people that belong in this community. They also need a way to pay for any problem that could happen, so Airbnb found an insurance company as business partner.

Now you know that to ensure the key activities that generate value to your client are well done so they work in your favor and not against you, you must have a great control and care of the resources you get for this to happen.

The Principles That Rule Your Business:

There is something your client is not going to manifest but is an unconscious thing that happens to everybody. They prefer a company with ethical values and sense of quality, so I suggest that you establish the principles that are going to rule your company by choosing and regulating the things that everyone who works there must know and follow.

To get the great results you wanted to be selfless for everybody, you must have these rules that will remember everyone how to take decisions and behave in any circumstance so the company won't lose the north in the path you chose.

I recommend having four or, maximum, five statements that are non-negotiable. For example, I am going to use Starbucks to keep showing how big companies have an excellent and selfless inspiringphilosophy instead of a limiting mission. Starbucks's philosophy is "to inspire and nurture the human spirit – one person, one cup, and one neighborhood at a time."

So, to get everybody (partners, employees, suppliers, etc.) into the behaviors and decisions that walk actions to get this result, they defined five principals:

- Principle 1: Make it you own.
- Principle 2: Everything matters.
- Principle 3: Surprise and delight.
- Principle 4: Embrace resistance.
- Principle 5: Leave your mark.

You can choose the principles you think would make your inspiringphilosophy achievable for everybody. In my case, I adopted three statements as the principles that will rule the inspiringphilosophy of my company. My inspiringphilosophy is: Help business owners that feel stuck to become the person who transforms their business to sell more, grow, and expand by inspiring the world. The principles I chose are:

- Principle 1: Work for incredible results.
- Principle 2: Encourage personal transformation.
- Principle 3: Generate value for others too.

Remember that these principles lead everyone who works for or has any kind of influence in my company to make possible the dream I have for my client.

Chapter Four:

Interest Them

You already created the best way to make your dream come true and help others making their life simple in some way, but you need your prospects to know about you and your value proposition.

Most of the entrepreneurs think that it is less expensive to hire someone to sell their products or services than making some advertising, but it is not true. Let me explain you why:

1. A person has a limited range; one person could reach X number of visits or calls in a certain period of time, so if you want to make more sales you must hire more people.

2. Outside, there are possible customers needing what you offer and maybe your people are not reaching them, but if you post some advertising, they can call you or go to your place to buy what they are looking for.

3. When you hire someone to help you open market, this person must be totally convinced about the good quality of the product or service that the company is offering and that the business could grow and guess what, the only person who fits exactly in the profile is you, the owner. So, you have to invest time and energy to make your sellers feel what you feel. This is why the most common complaint I hear when I work with the owners is that they are the ones who make the highest percentage of the incomes even if they have a group of sellers visiting and calling prospects every day.

The Marketing Plan:

To make these results different, you should start with a Marketing Plan. This doesn't mean you have to hire the most popular marketing agency or that you have to invest lots of money because I will show you how to do it right and simply.

The Marketing Plan you are going to create has two sides to focus on:

1. *Communicate to Prospects and Clients what is the value proposition of your company.*

If you communicate to your prospects and clients what the value proposition is of the product or service you offer when they are visited by your sales team, they will be happy to receive them.

Let me put a dramatic example here to make it clearer. Let's suppose that you are a pharmaceutical scientist, and after a lot of years of investigation, you and your team have discovered the cure for cancer. It is a very noble product. It is a natural remedy that kills all affected cells with no collateral damage in only a few weeks.

As the owner of the cure and a very clever person with a beautiful soul who tries hard to cure people, would you opt to hire some sellers to make some calls and go out there and find some possible clients, or would your good intentions lead you to make a massive communication so everybody in need around the world could be aware of the existence of the cure you developed?

Yes! I know that you would find out how to make the world know. Because you made this product to help, following a selfless philosophy. Regardless, you would make a great income not only for selling the cure but also for everything related to be well known in this profession.

I really believe that you have somebody's cure – your product or service is what someone is looking for, and you already designed it so well that is going to help many people. This is why you must make a marketing plan before you think about hiring some sellers.

Now, almost every important company invests in publicity but not in any kind of publicity. They invest in emotional publicity (for example: Coca-Cola, Huggies, Unicef). Maybe I just made you remember some good commercials – I love Super Bowl commercials. What these companies seek is to sensitize their public so they can create an effect. You will truly cause that same effect if you focus in following the seven steps of the INSPIRE Business Model I am teaching you now. All the marketing that you will do, although your economic capability is low, will cause that effect.

2. *Communicate to your Sales Team what is the value proposition for your clients and prospects and here*

> *you have to add what is the value proposition for your Sales Team, too.*

Most small and medium companies invest in marketing efforts to attract more clients and separately invest in recruitment efforts to get more and better workers, but I am going to tell you something most people don't know. A well-done marketing plan would work not only for the clients and prospects, but it is going to attract other people who want to help or serve the same cause as you. So, every marketing plan should start from the inside out. Nobody can sell something they are not convinced of. That is the secret of how MLM makes people sell their products only for a commission plan or a non-profit company has so many volunteers.

Well, to make it more explicit, I want to continue with the example we were assuming before. You, proudly, created this incredible product and let the world know about it. I'll bet that a lot of people will call to work with you. Some of them will want to learn from you and others want to serve the people with cancer that you are going to help. This reaction will bring only benefits for everybody: the client will have a gorgeous team attending his need, this team will be doing what they love, and you will be a happy leader.

Ok, to create this amazing way to get known by the people who are waiting for the product or service that you created, to help them or make their life simpler you should make sure you follow this advice:

1. Define the goals you want to achieve in short and long terms with the Marketing Plan.
2. Communicate your inspiringphilosophy.
3. Identify the best way to communicate so it gets to the audience you want to reach; if you figure this out very well you will save money and have awesome results.
4. Measure the results of the efforts you did in certain time.
5. Analyze the impact and make decisions.

The Commercial Plan

Now is the moment you can draw the roadmap to create an efficient sales department; when you are sure you have a company that can generate interesting incomes, and that makes a value proposition that your clients and prospects will know.

These are the steps you have to follow to draw the roadmap for your sales department:

1. You should know what is your "break-even;" remember that when you validate your business you already define key activities, resources, partners, and the cost of the structure you need to generate this value proposition.

2. Define the average of sales a seller could do in one day, and project it to a quantity of sales a seller could do in a month.

3. Determine how many sellers you need to achieve your break-even.

4. Define what is the life-cycle average of the product or service your company sells.

5. Specify what your company sales goals are. You must have two kind of goals: new clients and old clients buying again. If your company has historical achievement, let's start from there. The INSPIRE Program I created could make your sellers sell at least a twenty percent more than what they usually sell. I am going to keep showing you everything about this program while you finish creating all the conditions to make this more functional.

6.

Chapter Five:

Serve with Love

The inspiringphilosophy and the marketing plan is getting very good results, you are leading a group of people that are attending a lot of clients that love and need your product or service because it helps your clients make their life easier, but although everyone has the best intentions, you have to create the perfect atmosphere and culture to potentiate what all these good people can do. This is how you can create a culture of service and help.

The sense of help doesn't come or stays naturally. It depends on what kind of synergy your sales team is going to have. I recommend that you develop a culture of service following these four steps:

1. How are you, as the owner, going to serve your sales team?
2. How is your sales team going to serve each other?
3. How is your sales team going to serve your client?
4. How is everyone going to serve someone else that needs help and charity?

A company that thinks about everyone's benefit is a company that has better harmony and wins the will of the people.

The Owner as a Server:

It is a leadership style. Don't misunderstand. I am not saying that the owner has to be the one who works for everybody and be permissive with their employees. What I mean is that the owner is the person who can really inspire everyone and help them achieve their own purpose.

There are two things employees must have: good attitude and aptitude. Attitude is what we are seeking with the marketing plan, which is the interested that the person should show when working in your company, because the aim of the company is to help to solve a cause Aptitude is the capability these persons might have to get their job well done. With this premise, you can find four kind of employees:

1. *The ones that have a good attitude and aptitude:* Those are the ones you must give directions and let them know that you are behind to help them if they have any unexpected trouble. Make them part of the decisions and reward their performance.

In this profile fits perfectly a person who has enough experience and education to do a certain activity, but also this person is self-motivated to do her or his job well because he or she is dreaming to help the client or become X professional.

2. *The ones that have a good attitude and no aptitude:* Those are the ones you have to teach on how to do things, serve them with patience and hours of training. You must follow their improvement to find out if it is worth to keep them in the company. Here you have to give them the confidence to progress but let them know what the expectations are supposed to be shown in a certain period of time.

In this profile fits perfectly a person who just graduated, maybe has knowledge about the job but is very junior to do it right without supervision, even though he or she has all the desire to work in the company and become the person who can make his job correctly.

3. *The ones that have a bad attitude but a good aptitude:* Those are the ones you must serve with patience to inspire them on a bigger vision, or let them notice that they are not feeling right and they have to move somewhere else where they feel right.

In this profile fits perfectly a person who has all the experience and the education to accomplish his or her job perfectly but is tired of what he is doing. He feels like he is too much for the job position he has right now, and he is working there because he doesn't have more job opportunities for the moment.

4. *The ones that don't have attitude or aptitude:* Those are the ones that you have to serve with love and patience to make them notice that they have to work in another place.

In this profile fits perfectly a person that worked or studied for a different activity and doesn't like at all what he is doing for living now. Believe it or not, this is the highest percentage of the persons that work in a company because they are part of the family, friends, or referrals from one of them. Trust in me when I say that neither is doing you a favor because you have the worst kind of employee and that person is wasting time.

Sellers Serving Each Other:

There is nothing more efficient than a group of people working together to achieve a common objective. This is not a normal behavior, but it is the best way to make your sales department accomplish the goals your company needs to grow. To create this culture you have to set at least one goal to achieve every month that only can be done if everyone works together.

I am going to tell you that when I worked as a consultant, this was one of the services company owners used to ask about most: how to make them work together harmoniously and well-organized. That was how I used to sell a Team Building activity. But it only worked well when the group was out of the office and when I was the person in charge. Again, a non-long-lasting Consultant Companies service.

What I learned was that you don't need to contract a Team Building or any consultant process to make a group of persons work together as a high-performance team. What you really need is to set a goal. This goal should be well structured to motivate and mobilize everyone in the group so they want and need to work together as a team. While this is happening, you should act as the person who draws the roadmap to show them which is the best way to achieve the goal and inspire them so they walk the road with joy.

I am going to tell you a beautiful way I used to make my employees work very hard as a high-performance team to get done a demanding project. Once, my company was contracted by a government enterprise to recruit three specific profiles in twenty-one different cities in a two-week timespan. The candidates would pass through a demanding process with a very high score in their results.

When I accepted this job, I was thinking to myself that I was facing a great challenge, but they hired me because I was the only consultant company that showed them the capability to get these results. So, what I did was to organize all the work in a calendar so my team and I knew well what the steps were and that we had to do it in a certain time frame.

When I showed this calendar to them, the expression on their faces told me that it was a very ambitious project and that they didn't think that they could make it. I acted as a guide, telling them how the roadmap was well-designed so the work was able to get done. I reminded them that they were working for me because they were the best people in their profession and that I knew for sure that we could help each other. I knew that accomplishing this job was not a motivational goal for them, that in the middle of the project execution I was going to face a group of people stressed, tired, defeated, fighting with each other, and not meeting the goal.

I decided to make it simple; I was going to hire, at a very low price, a young publicist that wanted to do an interesting job to get known. I asked this young boy named Mario to help us cover our performance in the way to get this done. He showed us how to record ourselves and each other with our telephones so he could have videos of all of us when he could not be there to record. That is how we, as a team with all the help of Mario, created a very low-price social media marketing that made us reach the profiles we were desperately looking for. It was less cost this way than if I had paid for a publication in different media to only recruit these profiles. The group of people that was working for me were really focused in achieving the idea of being known because they were the best hard workers ever.

The work was made on time, and it was more profitable than I thought, so I decided to pass along the awesome video that Mario made for us in the social media, and asked people to donate some money to a poor community depending on how many likes or shares we got. The money was going to go as a help to a poor community that we met in a city where we have traveled to accomplish the recruitment process. Everybody on my team was very happy with this idea, and I was so proud of everyone. The community was very grateful, my client had a perfect service, Mario had a lot of fun, and I had lots of calls of new possible clients.

After this incredible experience, my team learned how to help and serve each other to accomplish a motivational goal for everybody. If I asked them to make something very demanding after, I never again saw that look and that expression of stress and fear I saw the first time. Instead their faces showed some agitation, emotion, laughs, and camaraderie.

Sellers Serving the Client:

Because we create a well-intentioned company and we hire well-intentioned people, we must develop a service policy based in your principals that your sellers and employees must follow, but it is very important that you should establish the client responsibilities to receive a good service. If you are into the differentiation strategy, the service you offer must be a whole experience.

Most of the time the client has the reason but not always. You may fall in an unattractive relationship where you, your staff, and your company are giving and doing everything that the client asks for – you must remember that you are going to have bunch of clients. Your client will be happy because he gets what he asks but unhappy because he will see you as a disorganized company.

Here are some of the basic things you must institute to make a service policy:

1. **Reaction times:** It is important that any contact that your sales team have with the client regarding his or her inquiries must have established response time.

2. **Communication:** The client must know the methods and the times they can contact the seller or someone at the company.

3. **Claims:** The client must know and have a way to manifest if something is going wrong with the product or service.

4. **Client Responsibilities:** The client should know that there are some conditions that make it possible to the seller and the company to give him a good service. Things like a certain anticipation time to make an order or to make changes.

And you should keep improving it with some feedback and data analysis.

The Company Serving a Minority Group:

If you want to grow, you must act like big companies do. Most big companies have generated helping programs for minority-needed groups. Call it karma, energy, or whatever you like, but when you help things go round, then it comes back in some way to you. A helping program could start from a small plan helping a nearby community. It is basically creating a helping hands program, and the donations could come from any volunteer worker or company. These kinds of activities should be done during the year. Most companies wait until Christmas or Thanksgiving festivities to help people, but at that time of the year is when all these communities are overwhelmed with good intentions.

A helping program is something that makes the team work together and could replace a team building activity.

Ok, do you remember the money I offered to give to this poor community my team and I as help? What we did was very transparent – we asked people on social media to share and give us a like, and we'd donate X quantity of money to the community. After we finished the work, I took all this money, and I asked my workers to help find friends and families that wanted to help too, and we bought food, clothes, medicine, etc. to give them in person. We went there with a plan of making them play and have fun. This activity was better than a team building. We had to get organized in every sense, follow rules, respect each other, and accomplish a new goal to help these people that are in need. Everybody had to give part of their time and a little contribution. They knew that I was not paying for their trip or help, that the money I offered was for those persons, and everyone had to pay for their transportation and food. Everybody was willing to do this contribution and happy to have an incredible and peaceful moment.

It's better if you can do a constant contribution, as there are people that need our help. You can use the same core of business to help others. For example, using the case we created where you were a pharmacy scientist, you know there are people who could pay for the medicine you created and there are others who do not even have money to pay for medicine. You are not a social company, but you could get some help from the government, from a non-profit company, etc. You all can get a way to give these people a diagnosis, attention, and cure. For that goal you can recruit volunteers. I think you could create a program for people who have recovered from cancer and who want to make a contribution and sponsor others or even go and help them. There are a lot of ways to give the world back in gratitude.

Chapter Six:

Engage Their Passion

Now that you are running a business that is a great offer for your client, you might need some help, so I am going to show you how to choose and retain the best people for the team you are building.

Let me set the steps you have to follow to manage your human resources:

1. Attract the best candidates.
2. Choose the best candidates.
3. Retain the best workers.

I want to make one thing clear here: None of these steps will work properly if the North is not well set up. That is why, although you hired the best recruitment company in the whole world, they could not guarantee that the person that they found for you would be happy to work at your company with the conditions you offer now. They could not predict if this person will produce what you need him to produce. So, if you have the North well set and you follow the steps I am going to share with you in this chapter, you could do the best recruitment process by yourself without incurring in unneeded expenses.

Attract the Best Candidates:

This is the start of all of the Human Resources processes, so if you can make that the best profiles want to work at your company, you can choose from the best options. But if it is totally the opposite and your company is the most unattractive place to work, you and anybody else can't make a difference. You have to develop the idea that your company is a kind of private club that only a few can go in.

Let's figure out the characteristics that a private club has. Think about an incredible private club you know, a place with interesting people that enjoy being part of a community that share the same interest (philosophy), a place where they can find a special social improvement and the benefits they need and want to achieve the goal that interest and gather this community. We should know that to be part of a club is the hardest thing because the more private a club is the more difficult it is to get in; the club has to choose you.

If you create an environment where people feel that they are joining a private club, that will be more attractive to them. If you could maintain this feeling when they become your employees, it is the best way to retain them.

Let me tell you an example. The atmosphere at the multinational company that I worked at had all the characteristics I want to show you in this chapter. When anyone wanted to apply to an open position, it was quite difficult for them to get in. There were so many applicants that the HR person had to follow a very exclusive procedure to choose the best candidate, and when someone successfully could enter to work in the company, he or she access to a world of exclusive benefits.

The company had an incredible place – the offices were equipped with the best furniture and everything else someone would need to work, surrounded with background music. At midday and evening there was a person who set a table with some bread, pastries, coffee, and other snacks so everyone who was hungry could eat. The restrooms were better equipped than the restrooms of a five-star hotel. When there were holidays, people from HR prepared a celebration in a very expensive restaurant and gave us all a present and a bonus. Two times a year, the company organized a family event: one for us to bring our families into the office so they could know about the job we do and how we help the company to achieve the goals, and another event where everybody, including their families, went out on an incredible trip to have a lot of fun with a luxury you can't imagine.

This was a high investment. I think the directors of the company did the correct numbers, and they decided to invest X percentage of the incomes to create and maintain this incredible atmosphere. While you keep reading, you will notice what were the savings they conquered. The first one you already noticed was that everybody would love to work there, so they didn't invest money and time recruiting candidates.

The other impact they made with this kind of labor environment was that everyone loved to work there, so everybody worked hard to get a good rate in the monthly performance evaluation. In two years, I never saw one person who had been fired or quitted because everyone really loved their job and made a good effort to continue working there. Personal turnover was very low.

To make your company attractive, you must have these activities happening constantly:

1. Share your company's philosophy. Remember we already designed a mission that makes somebody's life simple, so your marketing plan will have an effect not only with your actual and potential clients, but also with people who enjoy and know how to make this activity for living.

2. Share in social networks the projects you achieve with your workers. Projects like participating in contests, being part of a fair, traveling somewhere to make a promotion, etc. This is when you can use some advertising for the social help your company gives to a minority group and invite people in, who want to join this beautiful cause. You have to think of emotional and selfless projects you can share in social networks.

3. When you publish a vacancy, you must make some noise – make trivia or a challenge for the people who are interested in being part of your team or sales department so money is the second thing they might think about.

4. Make everyone who works or used to work at the company grateful. Remember the culture of service you developed. If you didn't think about serving your workers the right way when they were in your company and if you didn't make them understand with love and patient, the moment they go to work to another place, they could be mean and post negative things about you and your company, and nobody could have a nice ending with this.

Choose the Best Candidates

Before you choose the best candidates, you must know what you are looking for. Remember when Pedro didn't know how to describe the education and the characteristics of the person he needed when he was looking to hire his personnel? That is not a good signal. To choose a good worker you must have these things in mind:

Develop or Update the Profile

1. THE PROFILE: You must know how to describe the salesman who you are looking for. To make a good profile you have to define four important things:

    a. The Activities Description

- You should know and describe exactly what the activities of the sale position are. The more detailed the better.

b. The Studies Required

- Do the activities you described before need a special knowledge? Most of the commercial activities require more abilities or experience than a specific academic knowledge, but there are some products or services that need some instruction. For example, if your company sells computers, then you must hire sellers who have knowledge of computers and are a few years into their career.

c. The Experience Required

- Although you teach them everything about the business, it is better if the people you hire had worked in this before. That is how you can make sure that they know all the good and bad things that the position involves and you are relieved that they are not testing if they will like the job or not. So be aware that the people you hire have at least one year of experience.

  d. The Abilities Required
      •   The developed abilities make the sales-
          person do his work naturally, so you must
          specify what are the abilities that you ana-
          lyzed this position may need.

Develop an Assessment Center

  1. THE ASSESSMENT: You must contact only the
      people whose resume or information fits in the pro-
      file you create. The recruitment process for com-
      mercial areas not only requires an interview, but it
      entails creating an assessment center that consists of
      a roleplaying to watch how the candidates respond
      to a determined situation. You have to invent this
      case to make them figure out how to pass that situa-
      tion while you see them do it. This will prevent you
      from hiring people who have a good speech in the
      interview but do not do a good job.

  2. SENSE OF EXCLUSIVITY: Remember that your
      company is an exclusive club where only the right
      persons enter. If you could not find the person you
      are looking for, the one who follows your dream and
      have all the characteristics the profile requires, you

are not going to hire him or her, even though you are desperate. Believe it or not, it is cheaper to have an available vacancy than to hire anyone who does not go with the profile the company needs. That will make the people who get in very grateful and happy.

Retain the Best Workers:

This is another harder stage of the HR planification, but I am going to make it simple for you. You are now working with carefully selected profiles, and you don't want them to leave your company to run to another offer. To make them love where they work you have to follow these three steps:

Create a nice reward program.

You already hired some good candidates, and you have to have them motivated. That is something an MLM company does well, so we are going to take the basis of a very motivating rewarding program. This is built with three important aspects of a person's life:

1. Recognition: There is a simple way to do this. You have to create categories for different types of sellers depending on their performance, you can create a category A, B, C... or a category Gold, Silver, and Platinum, etc. so you can identify their achievements

to become part of a category that has different benefits. Sellers can go up and down in the categories every month, but at the end of the year, they can enjoy a celebration where they savor the status they have been more than X number of months in the year.

2. Economy: There is a basic salary and a variable remuneration that must be similar from what other companies pay.

3. Gifts: You can create some gifts during the year so that if someone achieves a goal you set beside the commercial goals that are already set, they can also have a gift. This is something you do only a few months during the year.

4. Family care: When someone works very hard, it is because they have to support their families, so you can give, once a year, a prize for the whole family. It doesn't have to be very expensive. It could be a dinner, or if you can and want, it could be something more expensive like a trip.

Make Your Leadership a Reason to Stay

I have worked for about eight years in recruitment processes and the first cause of people leaving their jobs is because they don't like their boss. I don't want you to pass through this kind of problem because you are investing time and money to make everything alright. So you should know that there are three kinds of bosses in the world.

1. Paternalistic Leadership: the ones who feel that they need to be loved by their employees, that hate the idea that someone is saying he is a bad person. This kind of leadership is the one that the leader ends up doing everything and is very permissive. A leadership like this doesn't end well with anybody. The workers have fun, but they feel like something is missing, that they could have more rewards if they have a better guide as a leader. I have seen how this leadership causes confusion and an environment of gossip and permissiveness in the company.

2. Bossy Leadership: This is the boss that every time he can have something to correct or to ask someone to do, it is very difficult to make this leader happy. Most of the time, he is making someone feel bad. I have seen how this leadership causes a lot of turnover and lack of commitment in the employees' behavior.

3. Directive Leadership: This is the one that guides the team to the goals they are chasing. This kind

of leader makes everyone feels confident to ask him anything, but at the same time, they know they have to come with solutions. This is a consistent person, someone who does what he says and acts in an ethical way. I have seen how this leadership is the one that generates the completion of big projects.

Create the Conditions to be Happy

Make the atmosphere of your office a nice place to be, put some music, give them good resources to make their job easy, allow them to put some family pictures on their desks give them time and space to rest their mind so they can go back to work again, equip a coffee room with good coffee and some healthy and good snacks, etc.

They will be so happy to work for the goals you set for them following the philosophy that gathers everyone.

Engage Your Clients

The best way to engage a client is buy engaging the good sellers that work for you because people don't buy to a company. They buy to a person, and that person could leave, taking your client with him to another company.

Once you have engaged your client through your good sellers, you can develop a loyalty or rewarding program according to the characteristics of your service or product.

In these eight years that I have being working training sales departments, I have seen some of this happening. For example, I worked recruiting workers for a great digital marketing company that was passing through the challenge of growing.

His principal owner wanted to leave the General Manager position. He thought it was time to hire a person for that position so he could move over to create another new business. The new General Manager he hired was a friend of his who had all the knowledge and experiences he needed in digital marketing, but he didn't have the ability to lead a group of people to manage a company, so what happened is that the people that worked there started to quit, and most of the clients they had followed the person who attended them.

The following year, after they invested in hiring a lot of people to replace the ones that were quitting, the new ones didn't last more than a few months. They lost most of the clients and lots of money. This behavior is clearer in services business, but it's a fact. People follow people, and relationships are very important.

Chapter Seven:

Refine Their Skills

A s Malcolm Gladwell described in his book *Outliers: The Story of Success*, to achieve excellence, you must have an accumulation of 10,000 hours of practice. This means ten years if you do the same thing twenty hours a week. What this chapter tries to demonstrate is that what Malcolm said is true unless you improve your learning and development by creating a community where you can teach and learn from each other.

What you need in your sales team is someone who achieves the commercial goals you set, but what you will find is that a few will hopefully make it and some others will not. You and other businessmen cannot wait until someone has accumulated ten years of experience. Here is the methodology I developed to make them learn from each other and for you to know what the weakest parts of your commercial activity are to help them get the results they have to make.

As I explained to you before, if you contract a trainer, even though he or she could be the best trainer in the whole world, the thing that will happen is that he or she will teach your team some steps or methodology someone invented to make more sales, but when your workers go back to their daily basis, they will not know how to put these steps in practice or maybe they will not remember all the steps they were taught. The worst of all is that you or other people at the office will make them go into the original method that everyone was using before. The sad part is that maybe you invested some money that will not return to you.

I am going to put a very clear and real example. One of my father's hobbies was to train dogs. Some of his friends and family asked him to train their dogs, and he did a very good job. He earned a lot of recognition at dog shows. Everything was perfect, but the problem was that the dogs responded better to the orders that my father gave them rather than to the orders that the real owners gave them. This happened because the dog responded to the leadership and how he taught him. The dog and my father made a connection where the dog knew the expectation my father had on him and my father knew exactly how to ask the dog to do something.

That was what happened when I worked as a consultant. I used to train the sales department to create the conditions and develop the abilities to make the people performance the way the company needed. When I was there, watching the people doing their job as I showed them, everything worked out very well. When I left them without my supervision for a long period of time, they went to a low performance again. That was why I developed the INSPIRE business program: to show the owner how to train their employees to do their work the way it had to be done to make the company grow and give everybody in return the benefits they are looking for.

To explain deeper what makes the difference between the traditional training and the program I developed, it is that I showed how the owners must train their staff. This is because they have the power to change the company's culture, but this is something no one could do immediately. This must be done little by little in a sustainable way. This program, as any other, only works with people that have the attitude and want to learn; that is why you must create the conditions to make them want to be part of your private club.

The owner must define what are the abilities that the person who covers a certain position must have to do well their responsibilities. This is not so difficult because, as an entrepreneur, maybe the owner used to do this activity before. In this book, we are focusing in the sales department, so I am pretty sure you have done the activities that a seller should do. You just have to detail what are the best practices and behaviors to make more sales and attend the clients as well as your philosophy promotes.

It is important that you act as a coach. You could go out with your sellers and show them what your client expects from the company. This is when you will obtain enough information to make decisions. You have been coaching and training your sales team, and you might have some economical increment results for sure, but you need to retain the employees that make you gain money and the ones who promote this beautiful and efficient culture you are creating to change your previous problems. To have the correct knowledge, you must transform everything that happens into analyzable information to make decisions.

The only thing that will bring you different and better results is to change the way workers do things and incorporate them as a habit in their daily routine. Here are my suggestions:

Each month you coach and assess the behaviors you have taught, so you are going to observe the ones you taught the first month, and the second month together, etc. That is how you change the culture and you create a habit.

When someone new starts to work in this area you need to show him or her to do what you have taught the rest because it is the culture that everyone is applying now. Be calm because you don't need to give him or her the knowledge little by little as you did with all the team before. Now it is the way everybody else does things, so it is in the culture of the company, and the new employee will see what everyone does and will imitate immediately.

Chapter Eight:

Normalize

The key of every change and good performance is the supervision. No one is going to change their habits unless you are behind them. The program that I am teaching you cannot be done without supervising what your employees do daily until they introject the standardized behaviors, and you, as the owner of your company, should have the good habit of controlling them too.

Formats and Statistics

While you disaggregate every ability in observable behaviors you might need some help to follow what everyone has to do. You will be tempted to register some of the things you showed them. For example, make them call X number of prospects every day and register the information they have. What you must do is create formats or documents that help your team to register important data you are going to control later. You have to socialize this document later with the rest of the company teams and to review it in the coaching time.

Here, you are going to learn another important activity that will bring more money to your company. It is to register the most information you can to make your company grow. I am going to give you three ideas of what you can register:

1. *Make your sellers ask for reference from your clients.*

I was looking to get a big company that produced tile as my client. I worked hard to have some meetings where I explained to them how my services will make them sell more. After a few months of talking, they told me to prove to them that what I did was really a good thing for them, so they gave me access to one of the stores they had. This was a store that had bad results. For almost half a year, the sales were below the fifty percent of the goal. They gave me two weeks to do my magic, and I realized that the main problem was that the government was doing some work on the street, and there was no access and nowhere to park.

The person in charge of the store and the sellers were waiting for people to enter and buy the products, but that way was not enough. I made them call every client they had attended in the last year and tell them about the promotions and ask for at least one reference to call. In about ten days we achieved eighty percent of the commercial goal for the month. I got the company to contract me, and I made them get to ninety-seven percent of the goal in the first month.

2. *Make your team create a document with all the complaints clients tell them.*

When I worked for this tile company, we grew so much in sales, but we also grew more in complaints. I made everyone register all kind of complaints we were having, and the conclusion we reached was that we had a problem with the logistic area. We increased sales but not the capacity at the warehouse, so our clients had the delivery out of time. We worked to solve this problem immediately.

3. *Make them register why a prospect did not buy some item or service.*

One of my biggest clients was a bank. This company had as a product a credit for people that ran a very small business with very low incomes in remote places. This big company also sold these people very good health insurance.

When I started working with them, I noticed that there were some people that didn't want the benefit of the insurance. I asked everybody to gather some data so we knew exactly the reason why we were not selling it to everybody. There were two reasons: the first one was that the sellers didn't know how to explain all the benefits that the insurance gave to the people, and the second one was that the insurance they sold didn't cover any non-professional health assistance, and the people in this community preferred to be attended by the local medicine man. After this important information, they developed a plan that included some attention to these kinds of cultural practices.

Let me tell you what you can do with that information:

1. Call the person your client referred and tell him about a promotion to convert him into another client.

2. If you have a document with all the complaints, you can identify where is your bottleneck in the company and fix it.

3. Most of the no's your seller receives are because the prospect you reach has another need or another way to buy. If you can see an opportunity in a big market, you can develop a product made for those needs.

Policies

The organizations and societies that grow fast are the ones that learn about the things that happen in any situation. As long as you register any kind of information, you can set some precedents and prevent or know how to act in different aspects. The most important and relieving thing you are going to realize is that you can make your employees make their own decisions. You will have more time to do things that really matter instead of running all the time to put out fires.

All the things you imagine that your team can register you can use to create a policy so everyone could know what to do in that situation. For example, you have a client who wants to buy your product with a wholesale price. He needs to know how many items he requires to buy to have this preference price. So, the seller tells the client to wait until he can reach you to ask what the client needs to know. It can be up to an hour later when you answer X number. If you have a registry of this, you can add this situation to a policy that has to be in a freely accessible place. Then when another seller has this kind of question, he can access this registry and find the answer immediately.

Technology

This is what every company chases – automatization. If you want things to be made perfectly, you should look for a system. Nowadays there are a lot of free or really cheap systems you can use to avoid errors.

Something else that is very important is that you and your team can work in the cloud. All the information they can collect and register should be in shared documents so it is easy for everybody to work on the same document and have the information updated and secure in a moment.

That is the way you can save money and avoid mistakes.

Chapter Nine:

The Big Obstacle

I already told you everything you should know to make your business grow. This is the most powerful way to do it because it is the long-lasting way. All the time and money that you are going to invest here is worth it. You will stop leaking money with the personal rotation, paying recruiters, consultants, or trainers. You will stop risking the future of the company, jeopardizing your client's satisfaction, and you will have an efficient sales team that is selling the number of products or services you set for them.

Now I am going to tell something you might know: There are some big obstacles you must confront to achieve the results you want to.

Start Doing It

This methodology covers lots of areas, and it is very normal to wonder if your business really needs all of that when you start. But let me tell you that if you really want to go from being the small business you have run for some years to a well-recognized company, you should stop doing what you have been doing and follow the steps I have showed you. The way to start it is to realize that your business has more potential than you can conceive right now and that you are holding yourself back from success by not making a decision. So, what are you waiting for? Every minute you wait is keeping you away from reaching out your dream.

When you start doing the five steps I explained, you are going to notice immediately that everything is going to change – even your excitement for the company that you've been keeping in a drawer.

So, don't jump any step because the others will not work the same way. Be prepared to do everything I said, and do it now. Tomorrow is going to be too late, and you will notice then.

I have seen how friends and clients waste lots of money waiting month after month until years have passed, thinking that something would happen. But nothing happens if you don't do it yourself.

Nobody Likes Change

When you start making changes in the company, almost everybody will be against it. Be prepared because when you implement the benefits, everybody will be very happy, but when you implement the rules, the goals, and the performance evaluations, you are going to hear all kinds of complains and excuses. It is normal. Remember that you are a leader who can serve with love and patience.

What I've seen in my ten years of experience is that the people with higher seniority are the ones who refuse change. What they are really looking for is to stay in their comfort zone. Even friends and family will try to turn you down because they are afraid to try something different.

This is a job that has to be done as quickly as possible because wrong things happen. Things change. You could be losing a big client or a big opportunity, and everything you have done is wasted or even worse – somebody in your industry does it first, gains a good portion of market share, and starts growing quickly.

Make everybody help so they can be part of the process, and they'll know the reasons why you have made some decisions.

You Will Doubt Your Leadership

While you make changes and give orders and some of them complain, do not lose your strength. This only will make you lose time. Remember that you are the one who built the company and your dream is what drove you and anybody else where you are now. You just have to adjust your leadership to the new situation you have to endure for a while.

Remember Pedro? He knew that this was the solution he was looking for. He was wasting time and money until he discovered that he was the only one in charge of his results. When Pedro started to make some changes at the beginning, people resisted – including family and friends. Everyone wanted to make some comment about what he was doing and make him doubt the decisions he was taking. But he stuck to the plan and got the results he was expecting.

You Will Not Have Time

Let me tell you that you, like anybody else, don't have enough time. Everyone is doing a lot of things during the day. Maybe you have more responsibilities besides the company, like a family or studies, and I am pretty sure that you are the one that keeps the boat afloat and puts fires out. But your boat is sinking very slowly and quietly. You may not notice, so you should make a pause on what you are doing now and do something to fix your boat and make it faster.

This digital marketing company I told you about that hired a new general manager. They were desperate because they were losing all their clients, so they chose to contract recruitment and consultancy companies. I believe that they invested more than what they were earning to solve this problem. They lost time, and at last, they finished when everything collapsed. If they would have taken their time to learn how to solve this by themselves, they would have not lost so much money and time, and they could become the people who could solve any situation every time they needed.

When you achieve the implementation of this practical system, you will be the one that empowers everyone to keep paddling while you guide them to the treasure.

This Method Takes You out of Your Comfort Zone

When you pass through the stages that the program requires, you could face some different emotions that will go up and down. This is totally normal and good to make your head now perceive problems that you haven't seen before and find solutions to them. After you achieve the right solutions, you will feel relief and joyful. To change the way your company works, I need to change your way of conceiving, doing, and wanting things. It is not easy – nothing good is. You are going to reinvent your working model and reinvent yourself. Life will bring you what you were asking for all this time, a big and profitable company.

Everybody Will Win

This program will bring happiness to everybody: you as the owner and every worker and client you have and will come to have. Your effort and commitment will make a difference in everybody's life.

Chapter Ten:

It's Your Time to Make It Happen

I started my consulting business when I noticed that services like recruitment, training, and consultancy didn't work in long term to make a company sell more, so these three services turned into a sunk cost. I realized that what makes a company increment sales is to develop a growth culture and to make a change in the culture the owner has. This takes seven steps.

Start with a dream of a business that makes somebody's life easier, define the philosophy, then analyze the industry to find out if it is a good investment or otherwise define a strategy to make it interesting. Validate the business model to establish a value proposition so you can create an emotional marketing plan for internal and external people and set the goals for the commercial plan.

Make everybody else live easier by creating a service culture where you as the owner and the head of the business help your employees to work with aptitude and attitude in your company, or let them go to where they feel better. Create situations and a culture where all the workers serve each other. Create a policy of service for the client to know and respect, and finally, offer some external help with a helping hand program.

A well-thought human resources activity will bring effective results so when you attract the right professionals you can choose to make them demonstrate that they have the capacity to make a good performance. Now you know that you have to formalize the salesperson profile so you can train and evaluate your members to seek which one are you going to retain.

I taught you a long-lasting methodology to create a culture where you make your sellers develop the abilities you disaggregate in observable behaviors to teach and coach them what and how to do things to increase sales.

Formalize formats to get all the information you can and turn it into a new product or service. Develop policies so your team will not have to wait for you to make decisions.

After doing this, you will be running a company that is ready to grow, and you make sure it is growing since you took the decision to start this program.

Acknowledgments

I would like to thank my daughter, who inspires every day my personal and professional growth, my father who always has supported me and gave me an incredible example of constancy and perseverance, and the love of my mother, her wise advice, her patience and care.

I would also like to acknowledge all the teachers, clients, friends, and professionals that taught me important things in life.

To the Morgan James Publishing team: Special thanks to David Hancock, CEO & Founder for believing in me and my message. To my Author Relations Manager, Bonnie Rauch, thanks for making the process seamless and easy.

Many more thanks to everyone else, but especially Jim Howard, Bethany Marshall, and Nickcole Watkins.

Thank you to Angela Laura and the team of The Author Incubator.

And, above everything, thank you to my Lord.

Thanks to all of you for being a part of my life.

Thank You!

I am so happy you finished reading *Inspire*; the fact that you are now at the end of the book tells me that you are ready to become the person who can manifest an inspiring philosophy to shift your small business into a growing company.

I am the most passionate person to help you make this happen in the fastest and the easiest way. I am going to share with you a master class where I will teach you everything you should know about *Inspire* and the tools you will need while you go through this journey. Enroll for *free* by visiting the online learning center at www.inspirebusinessprogram.com.

The tools you will find there will help you understand:
1. How to analyze the industry
2. Business validation
3. Commercial plans
4. Skills and observable behaviors
5. Coaching evaluation
6. How to develop a sales profile
7. Service policy format

If you think you need help, or if you have questions, please feel free to ask me by sending an email to info@inspirebusinessprogram.com.

I'm happy to share this inspiringphilosophy with you!

Yazmín Torres Padilla

wwww.inspirebusinessprogram.com

About the Author

Yazmín Torres Padilla, MBA. MSL., is the creator of the INSPIRE Program for generating a long-term culture of development workers' and leaders' skills with measured impact.

Her interest in solving most common organizational problems since 2010 has made her find the key to measuring the impact of training workers, developing a leadership culture, increasing sales in a sustainable way, and decreasing rotation with her INSPIRE Program.

Her international professional preparation in Ecuador, Cuba, Spain, and Thailand in the areas of Psychology, Business Administration, and Leadership make her master the field of diversity and strategy.

She has worked for ten years for recognized international companies of all types of industries, helping them with HR Consulting Processes like Evaluate the Organizational Climate, Develop Policies and Procedures, Performance Evaluation, Develop Profiles for type of positions, Training for Skills Development, Leading Recruitment Process applying Psychological Tests and Assessment Center, Corporate Governance, Create the HR and the Commercial departments, Develop a Correct Leadership Structure, etc.

On a personal level, she has an authentic search for spiritual growth and the eagerness to help others that has led her to be in a constant service attitude. That is what has motivated her to work with small or medium family companies and entrepreneurs, helping them grow by establish and implementing the INSPIRE Business Program.

She lives in Quito, Ecuador with her family.

Website: www.inspirebusinessprogram.com

Email: info@inspirebusinessprogram.com

Facebook: http://facebook.com/yazmintorrespadilla
Linkein: www.linkedin.com/in/yazmintorrespadilla